Finding Her Being Her

A Journey of Poems

Finding Her Being Her

A Journey of Poems

Nilam Patel

www.findingherbeingher.com

Illustrations and cover design by Nilam Patel

ISBN: 979-8-218-22535-3

For my husband,
daughter
and son.
For my earth,
sun,
and moon.

Table of Contents

If I'm still thinking of you
after today,
you'll turn into poetry;
which chapter you'll live in,
is up to you.

Chapter 1. Finding Her

Without a woman's
strength,
courage,
and love,
god himself
would not
exist.

Finding Her Being Her

While boys play,
girls will clean,
while men relax,
women will cook,
while brothers study,
sisters will serve,
while fathers are praised,
mothers will be judged,
while husbands work,
wives will give up passions,
but while the male mind is simple,
the female mind remains complex,
and while gods gloat,
goddesses will
create
entire
universes.

How is a
woman
who is
responsible for
creating life,
creating a home,
creating love,
not worshipped
like anything but
a goddess?

Why is it so difficult to
take care of ourselves,
at least as much
as we take care of
everyone else?

Our bodies have hearts,
but our minds have souls.
Our bodies make the change,
before our minds break the habit.
Our bodies are no longer in pain,
but our minds remember our cries.
Our bodies dance to the tune,
while our minds question the lyrics.
Our bodies act in haste,
while our minds tread softly,
for delicate wounds can heal,
but scars are never forgotten.

Finding Her Being Her

We doubt our abilities,
giving others a chance
to praise us.
We question our instincts,
waiting for others
to save us.

Nilam Patel

Every move questioned,
every question dismissed,
knowing what's best for me
without knowing me at all.

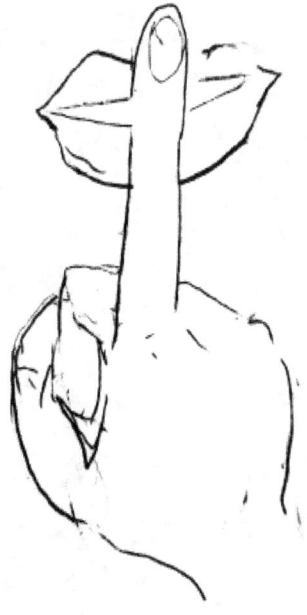

Finding Her Being Her

Surround yourself with people
that believe in your dreams,
even when you give up.
Spend time with those
that remind you of your passions,
even when the rest of the world
makes you forget.

The hand you nonchalantly
rested on my thigh,
haunts my thoughts
to this day.

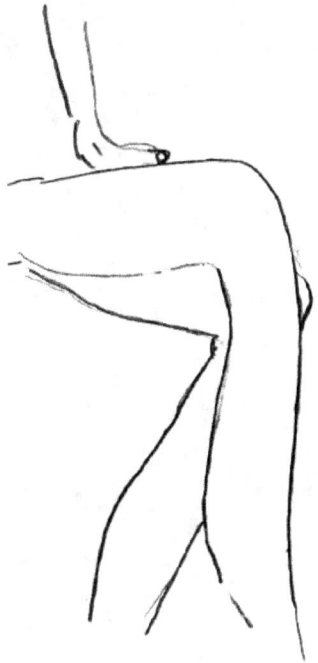

Finding Her Being Her

When we dismiss red flags,
we ignore ourselves,
when we welcome toxicity,
we stop believing,
when we tolerate disrespect,
we forget what love feels like and
when we accept less than we are worth,
we begin living in someone else's dream.

Nilam Patel

When you've never tasted love before
you make up recipes for it.
Without knowing the ingredients,
you imagine the flavor and how it's served;
but right when you think you've found it,
you take your first bite and
discover you've mistaken it
for poison.

Finding Her Being Her

The world tricks us into thinking
we have to be busy to be successful;
that ambition can only be related to
a career or wealth.
Let's accept ambition to also mean
a balancing act of all of our worlds
that includes the intangible luxuries
that most do not think they have control of;
a warm home,
a close family,
time for passions,
being mentally present for others,
or time to be with your own thoughts.
Know when to stop and just be,
rather than constantly
thinking about what is next.
You may have already achieved it,
only to continue walking past it.
Letting others define your goals
will only leave you
chasing after a dream
that was never yours.

She felt like a ghost,
walking around
in a world that existed
without her.

Finding Her Being Her

She embraced her
deepest weakness,
held its delicate hands,
and as she cared for it,
it became her
greatest strength.

Nilam Patel

She laughed and danced
under the peach sunsets
she had once called home.
She was carefree and breezy,
not thinking of the sunrise
and what was soon to come.

Finding Her Being Her

She mingled, chatting away,
unveiling her deepest secrets,
trusting others, before
trusting herself.

We lower our gaze
when facing the sun;
it can spark our flame
or burn us
to ashes.

Finding Her Being Her

Expect little from others and
the smallest favor will
resemble life's greatest gift,
while the deepest betrayal will
remain someone else's mistake.

Nilam Patel

I thought you were
what love looked like;
I showed your picture
to everyone I met,
only to find out,
I had been unveiling
my very own kryptonite.

Finding Her Being Her

and then she realized
he could never be
the reason she danced,
the reason she smiled,
the reason she loved,
for he was struggling
to figure it all out
himself.

Nilam Patel

She had a whole vibe
when she walked in.
I wanted to know her,
I wanted to be her,
I had so many questions;
and in the end,
it was my reflection in her eyes
that gave me all my answers.

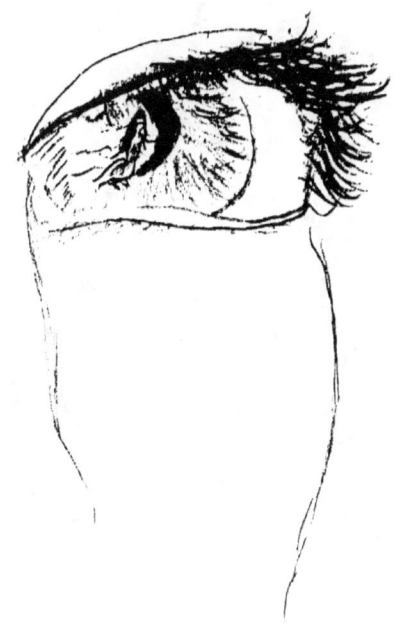

Finding Her Being Her

Seek to understand them
so they can love you fiercely,
the only way they know how;
and it is then,
you will be understood.

She was not too much,
she was just enough;
and the place she felt understood,
was one she'd never leave.

Finding Her Being Her

She asked you
to come prepared,
she was never here
to teach.

-if only you heard her

Red flags
are not suggestions,
they are
bright,
flashing,
lights;
and each time they are ignored,
is another moment lost,
to prepare for
what's
sure
to
come.

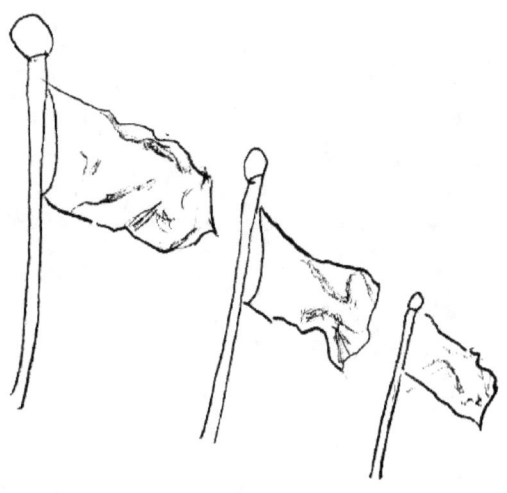

Finding Her Being Her

To live,
trying to find
yourself in others,
is a life wasted.

Nilam Patel

We must be brave enough
to say no
in a world that walks in,
expecting yes.

Finding Her Being Her

Once you embrace
the stillness of solitude,
deep in your thoughts,
surrounded by peace,
you will choose to spend time with
only those that are worthy.

Some days, she'd look up,
to admire them, soft and gentle,
cottonlike, her favorite;
and on others, his, spread effortlessly
like abstract strokes across the sky.

Whenever they appeared,
she'd remember him;
wherever he was,
she'd stop and smile.

She loved him through the heavens
and as they glided over in gray,
she'd think he was gone;
but the day would come she'd see
both dashes and dollops of white
and she'd feel him,
closer than ever.

Finding Her Being Her

Under a somber sky,
a young girl will always
wonder why she is different;
lead her past the clouds
to dance with the stars and
show her how she too, shines.

Nilam Patel

and we accept,
we must make room
only for those we can
call home.

Finding Her Being Her

Under the night sky,
her spark flames into a passion,
delicate, but fierce;
needing to be fed and fueled
in that moment, there and then;
for as dawn awakens,
it may begin to wither
and the dream itself,
will be forever lost.

Her pain was her own;
she experienced it early,
when no one knew
she had the complexity to feel sorrow;
the journey raised her to be unbreakable
for she had lived the hell and still returned.
She longed for stillness now,
exhausted and empty,
she wanted to be filled;
but this time with simplicity,
rustling leaves, crisp air, dusky skies
and all the things she could not admire,
locked in the depths of chaos.

To be the woman you've
been searching for in all the wrong places,
you must first find her within.

Don't slouch,
sit up straight.
Don't laugh out loud,
cover your mouth.
Don't talk so much,
answer when asked.
Don't relax,
cross your legs.
Don't dream big,
be practical.
Don't ask for help,
figure it out.
Don't act like a man,
be a woman.

-the worst and best lessons

Finding Her Being Her

Her best smile
could never hide
the pain in her eyes,
the havoc of her heart,
the tragedy of her thoughts,
silently crying out for help.

She was quiet
but never shy,
she would smile
but never laughed,
she would move
but never danced,
she was told
but never asked.

Finding Her Being Her

As she starts her story over,
if she makes you a character,
know she has chosen you
to help lay the bricks to her future.

Nilam Patel

When given a stream of choices
recognize when you're prepared
for the hard road and
when the easy one is
the only way you'll survive.

Finding Her Being Her

She learned one person
could never be
magical enough
for all her needs,
that we are not divine
but mere beings living
in a cruel but forgiving world;
and it was then, she was able
to accept
and be accepted,
to embrace
and be embraced,
to love
and be loved.

Nilam Patel

A word
overloaded with syllables
she could not say
and endless meanings
she could not convey;
but after all,
love is felt,
not spoken.

Chapter 2. Being her

Wrapped in a series of
checklist items,
motherhood
stops us in our sprint
to life's finish line,
to take a breath
and notice,
we are actually
running a marathon,
that's worth
slowing down for.

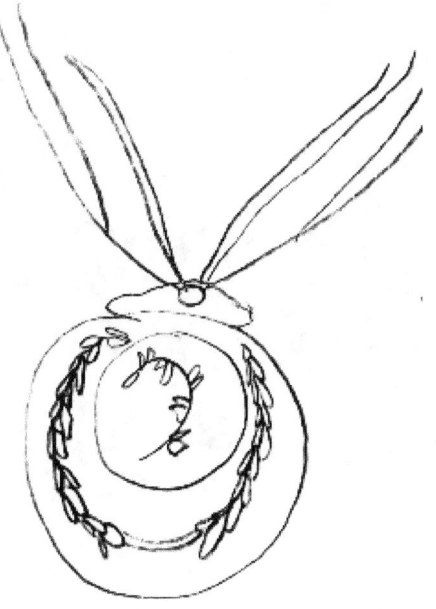

The idea of motherhood
is an idea stolen;
for therein lies the fear,
that one day,
women will have
the audacity to think,
any of it is our decision.

Motherhood,
is a lifelong path
we choose to take,
filled with endless mistakes,
that are ours to make.

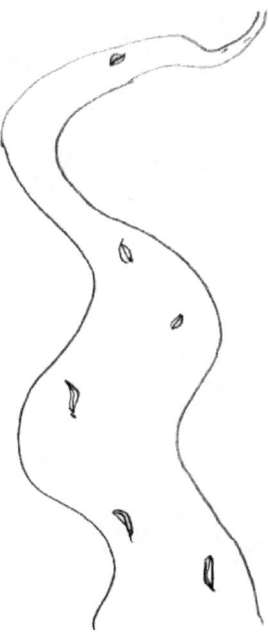

The vulnerability of
those tiny hands
fill our thoughts
and as we fight to protect them,
we lower our own guard.

-the battle of mothers

How do we handle grief
that others do not feel?
How do I honor a life
that no one knew,
but me?

Finding Her Being Her

No one will tell her
they are proud;
all she does,
is simply expected.

I was naive
to think
I alone
could protect her.
I was hasty
to dream
of her life,
all before she had
seen the sunrise.

To have a
daughter
is a privilege;
for those that
are chosen,
raise our
future.

Why do we band together
to celebrate the rainbows,
after leaving mothers
alone to mourn the storm?

Finding Her Being Her

We finally see our mothers
the moment we become
mothers ourselves;
wide-eyed and in awe,
we wonder
if we will ever
match up.

Grief stops you in your tracks,
but stops at nothing;
it leaves only when it's ready
and explains itself to no one.

Finding Her Being Her

She never understood grief,
with moments of bliss
glazed with guilt,
bursts of sorrow
wrapped in joy,
but it was hers to feel.

Despite the strong and brave shades
we often feel we need to paint of a woman,
it is rather her humble and soft hues
that make her glow, even when they try to
burn

      her

         down.

They bring us down
because otherwise,
we would have an unfair
advantage.

We become a mother
the moment
we feel the need
to love silently and
raise our shield
to the world.

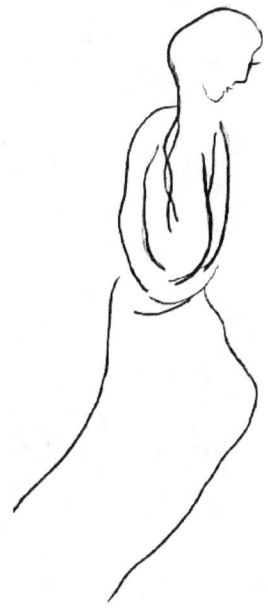

Finding Her Being Her

Like each one before us,
when we learn we are stronger
than they want us to believe,
we can begin our own revolution.

Hands folded,
head bowed,
she prays for
those around her,
but never
herself.

Finding Her Being Her

Before we give up trying to
save the world,
let's start with our
teachers, neighbors, heroes
and see how far we get.

Nilam Patel

Motherhood
is a foreign world
you enter without a map.
Upon arriving, many greet you
but do not stay;
and after searching and wandering,
you can't seem to find the village
everyone told you about.

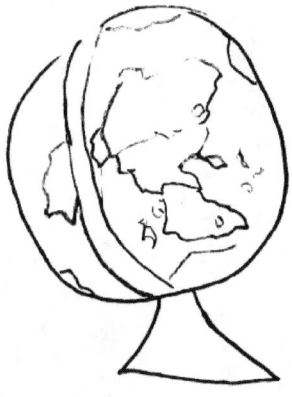

Finding Her Being Her

Our children deserve to
see through their mothers
all the things women need and
witness through their fathers
how they should be given.

The first time
her daughter looked up at her
with unwavering eyes of adoration,
she slowly melted into the earth
and returned a goddess.

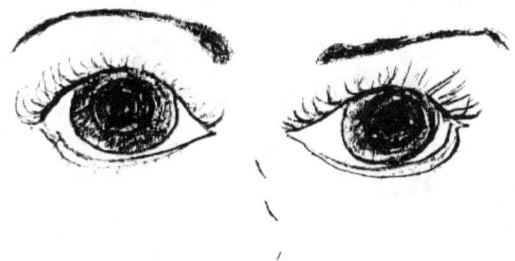

It is only where
sorrow exists,
does joy have a
chance to shine.

When both your worlds break,
lean on each other;
you are stronger together
and just as you need their shoulder,
remember to catch them
before they fall.

Finding Her Being Her

It is the hint of a smile
that becomes a laugh,
the slightest touch
that becomes an embrace,
the smallest act
that becomes your whole world
and the start of a friendship
that becomes your greatest love.

Grow together and you will
always have their ear,
evolve together and you will
always hold their hand,
cry together and you will
always wipe their tears,
love together and you will
always have their heart.

The hardest
no
is the one that
protects us.

She was labeled a superhero
when she spoke of her struggles.
She was congratulated
when she wanted to be heard.
She was handed a medal
when she asked for peace.
She was lifted onto a pedestal
when all she needed was someone
to walk in her stride,
to hold her hand,
to see her.

- why weren't you listening?

Finding Her Being Her

The sacrifices
and heartache
a mother endures
are some of her
deepest secrets;
not expected to struggle,
not encouraged to share
and when it's too late,
they wonder why
no one ever knew.

-the taboo

Nilam Patel

As she sat along the shore,
each wave poured over her,
soaking up the struggles it could;
when it couldn't hold any more,
it peeled away, carrying them with it,
leaving her longing for the next one.

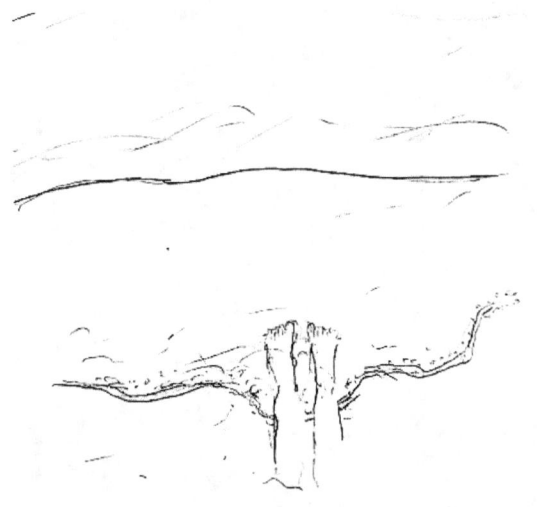

Finding Her Being Her

The ashes themselves
told the story,
equally sacred and harrowing;
and as she watched them
softly float into the abyss,
she silently prepared for the day,
she would see them again.

Nilam Patel

She was ever so alluring,
floating by effortlessly,
speaking with poise,
a magical force to know;
but as she walked closer,
only those that stayed, noticed
the crack in her voice,
the pain in her eyes,
her wistful aura,
her tired shoulders, on which
she carried the world.

To underestimate her
kindness for weakness
was the first mistake;
her icy eyes,
her fake smile,
hidden, but always there,
along with her wrath,
ready to burn it all down.

She spoke softly
so no one could hear,
she moved like a feather
not knowing which way to steer;
not realizing those around her
marveled at her voice and sway,
she tiptoed around
whispering all her secrets away.

Finding Her Being Her

She is not asked,
but forever told.
She is not masked,
but forever bold.
She does not cry,
but hides tears.
She does not pry,
but hides fears.

Nilam Patel

She accepted sadness,
so she could truly feel,
she welcomed happiness,
so she could fully heal.
One without the other,
waiting to finally meet,
is an in between state
longing to feel complete.

Finding Her Being Her

She will break her chains
when she's ready,
the magic words
always in her mind;
and when she says them,
she will resurface,
don't rush her,
give her time.

Nilam Patel

She taught her daughter
how to be kind to others,
over and over until
it became a habit;
and as she watched her
become a woman, she realized
she had never shown her
how to be kind
to herself.

Finding Her Being Her

Grief
sensed she had given it
all she could for now;
it floated away letting her
live and smile,
gather and strengthen
for a time,
before returning to
ask for more.

She is the hero,
in the shadows,
not bold enough
to be noticed;
she faces the flames,
letting the world choose
how much of her
it wants to see.

Finding Her Being Her

You are the answer
before they ask,
you are the healer
before they hurt,
you are the glue
before they break,
you are the mother
before they call,
and I see you.

-the only gift that was ever needed

She thought she
could pour herself
more and more into
the life expected of her;
and just as her last drop
reluctantly rolled down,
she looked inside and
there was nothing left.

-parched

Finding Her Being Her

A daughter sees her mother
as a mythical creature,
unable to make mistakes,
not allowed to fall;
but as she steps into the same shoes,
she finally sees her mother
as a woman trying her best
to live through it all.

The world is backwards
as if it's trying to trick her;
she waits for someone to
yell it's all one big joke
so she can exhale.

-she's still waiting

Chapter 3. Loving her

She existed in her own
fairy tale;
she was her own
greatest love story.

Finding Her Being Her

An evening with a group of close ones
brought intimacy,
an hour with her best friend
brought comfort,
but a moment with her thoughts
brought peace.

The first hints of gray
wrapped in disbelief,
the first glimpse of wrinkles
filled with questions
are difficult to accept;
but the first signs of wisdom
adorned with gratitude,
the first moments of peace
trimmed with grace
are gifts she'd waited
her whole life for.

-aging

Finding Her Being Her

Once you love
yourself
more than anyone
else,
you are finally
free.

Take time to admire
the woman staring back at you,
for she is not anyone
you have seen before,
and she may look different
tomorrow.

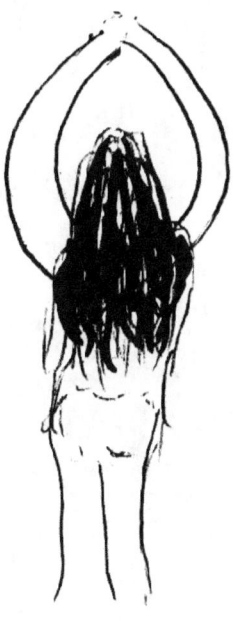

Finding Her Being Her

It is only
when you learn
how to love yourself,
can you teach others,
how you want to be loved.

When our
mind
body
and spirit
are all finally connected,
we will stop at nothing
to preserve
the feelings
of our own warmth
and delicate touch.

She used her turmoil
to make
the unimaginable
a reality.

Nilam Patel

Once you know
what peace feels like,
trust you will
find your way back,
after straying into the
chaos.

Finding Her Being Her

Why tell her
how she should,
when she could,
what is good,
she wants
great.
Why show her
how it's hard,
a different card,
to be on guard,
she accepts
fate.

The moment you start to
love your whole self,
is precisely the moment
you are
born.

Finding Her Being Her

From a blinding dark state,
in a cold, locked cell,
hate screams.
Spreading its wings,
over those seeking warmth,
love beams.
Let's free ourselves and
see how in flocks,
we soar.

The softest cashmere throw,
the warmest cup of chamomile tea,
the most comforting smell of baked bread,
the most soothing jazz tune,
the most relaxing yoga flow,
the slowest ocean wave weaving through our toes,
the gentlest sound of summer rain,
the stillest walk through nature,
will never compare to the
feeling of finding serenity
wrapped in our own embrace.

Finding Her Being Her

Let today
be the day
you fall
madly in love
with
yourself.

Art,
is the tiny glimpse
we give others
of our thoughts;
too sacred to speak,
too delicate for words.

Secrets
1. Your life is a sum of your choices
2. If you speak up, you will be heard
3. Eating healthy is eating normally
4. Saying hello to every part of your body should be part of your daily routine
5. Grooming includes nurturing how you feel
6. Never ignore your body's cues
7. Feel what you feel and never hide it
8. Learn how to cry
9. There are no roles, there is only one family
10. It is okay to love yourself
11. Make time for your friends, you chose each other
12. Call, don't text
13. Decluttering your home will declutter your life
14. It is okay to be bored
15. Schedule some weekends to have nothing scheduled
16. Stop at nothing to keep your peace
17. Stay minimal and you will have more
18. Find the calm and run from chaos
19. Never ignore the red flags
20. Say what you are thinking and apologize if needed
21. Say yes and figure it out later
22. Always demand respect and know when to leave
23. No one can silence you but yourself
24. Expect little
25. Drink water

Nilam Patel

In a world that is
black and white,
she paints in gray undertones
and gets away with it.

Finding Her Being Her

Let's go back to the days when
a bit of sunshine and love,
were the only cures we needed.

You are not
anyone's prey.
You are yours
to enjoy,
to savor,
to relish,
any way you like.

Finding Her Being Her

and just like that,
from behind the gray,
the sun hit my face.
I was living in color
and dreaming,
once again.

When she uncovered
that her beauty
did not depend
on another person,
it was the first time
she flew.

Our mind
is ours to
plant,
grow,
water,
nurture
and
love.

Don't underestimate what
a glass of wine,
an hour of laughter,
a series of stories,
an unload of emotions,
with a girlfriend,
can accomplish.

Our existence depends on
powerful women;
let's nurture them,
let's meet them,
let's protect them,
let's be them.

Her home
was simplicity,
a familiar voice,
a soft blanket,
a warm cup of tea,
a gentle touch,
a soothing melody,
a calming thought,
a relaxing book.

Finding Her Being Her

Calm your mind,
find her.
Honor your body,
be her.
Take your journey,
love her.

-read it again

Nilam Patel

Find that beat that
makes you soar
and play it
on repeat.

She couldn't find the thing
she'd been looking for,
so she decided
to make her own.

She became
her own muse;
and then,
a sensation.

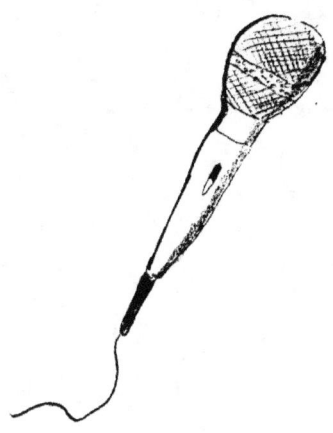

and like so many times before,
he looked down and asked,
"who do you think you are?"
bringing her gaze to his,
piercing and suddenly sure,
she answered,
"a woman."

Yoga is
the balancing,
the strengthening,
the oiling,
the decluttering,
the cleansing,
the loving,
the swirling,
of our mind
and body.

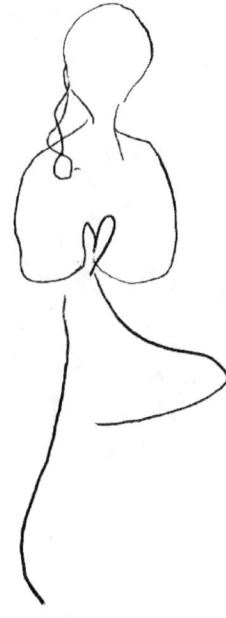

Finding Her Being Her

Not everyone gets a ride or die,
growing up and growing old,
a rare gift, ironclad and true;
so when she calls, come running,
in the moment, don't think,
just be there, take to the road,
and as you know, it's sure
to be one hell of a time.

Head hung,
dipping one toe in the water,
she saw a familiar face along the ripples
and remembered who she was;
as she placed both feet back on the ground,
she raised her gaze to the light and
dove in.

-she had always known how to swim

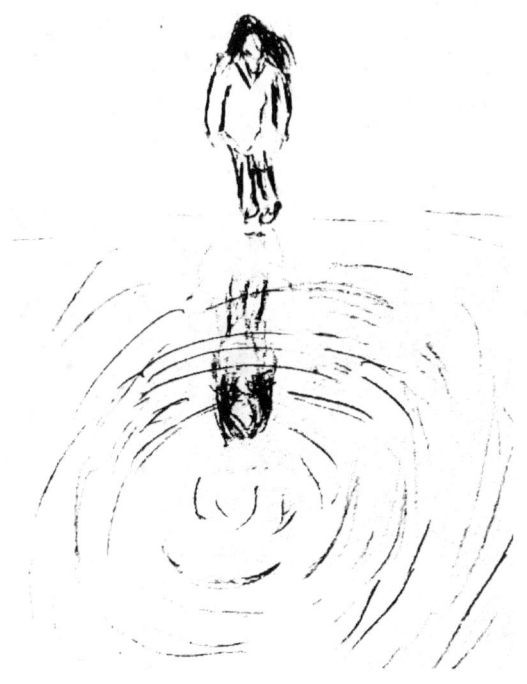

She needed things
she'd never ask for,
she wanted things
she'd never take;
she'd dream of the one
who'd give them all to her,
until realizing she was
her own to save.

Never knowing which way
she should run towards;
knowing the answer will
change again tomorrow,
worrying about
someone else's ideas
more than her own;
too quiet, too loud,
too lazy, too ambitious,
too sensitive, too strong
for them, but standing still,
perfect for herself.

Finding Her Being Her

When she speaks, hear her
when she loses, help her
when she hurts, heal her
when she falls, save her

-inner mantra

She lived in
an abstract world,
feeding off
morsels of asymmetry;
she was at ease
on an imperfect day,
never yielding to the rules,
a room full of flaws was home.

Finding Her Being Her

Take a deep *breath*,
a voice said;
she'd given in to mediocrity,
given up on glory,
but just as she glanced over,
she was finally left *breathless*.
As their eyes met,
he answered her questions,
cleared her darkest clouds,
found everything she had lost,
all in one moment,
one look,
one act
and for first time
she *exhaled*.

Just as the last leaf floats down and the earth rests,
we also need a moment of respite;
for when the season full of fragrance arrives,
we will emerge spreading seeds of hope.

Finding Her Being Her

She arrives bare,
unmade, undone,
she floats in waves
of simplicity and
shades of neutral,
she looks timeless,
modest, muted;
she is home.

Nilam Patel

Don't thank us,
walk with us.
Don't fear us,
see us.

Best regards,
Women

Finding Her Being Her

Strutting into our 20s,
we are told to be exhilarating.
Moseying into our 30s,
we are taught to worry about our timeline.
Stumbling into our 40s,
we are warned that we are replaceable.
Strolling into our 50s,
we are trained to be discarded.
Wandering into our 60s,
we are left to feel burdensome.
We learn to fret about each stage
throughout our journey;
but it is when the end nears,
in the depths of solitude,
we feel more alive than ever.

-the final act

In your hands is my journey, my inspiration and my hope.

When I first started writing poetry it was for the sole purpose of healing. A deep trauma that I had never fully dealt with resurfaced and opened up all the scars I had halfway sewn up years ago. After I wrote my first poem, they just kept coming until writing became a large part of me and who I am.

I set out to finally share my work and was overwhelmed with the sense of community I found. I never realized there were so many individuals out there like me. We are a small niche, but a special one that spreads passion, hope and most of all love.

My words and art are meant for healing and talking about the things that we often keep hidden. They were created to start conversations and invoke deep thought.

Let's continue to support each other and lift each other up any time we are starting to lose our spark.

Let's be kind to others but most of all, let's be kind to ourselves.

All the love.

Nilam is an artist and poet that is passionate about bringing awareness to topics that are often seen as taboo in today's world. As a Doctor of Pharmacy who advocates for both mental and physical health, she set out a decade ago to inspire and lift others through her words and art. She currently resides in Austin, Texas with her husband, daughter, son and pup.

Follow Nilam on Instagram @**nilam.poetry** for more.

Subscribe and Shop
www.findingherbeingher.com